GOLD RUSH ADVENTURE

by Linda Lyngheim

illustrated by
Phyllis Garber

Langtry Publications
Van Nuys, California

FOR CAROL, KEN, KEVIN, KRISTEN, AND KOLLEEN

Library of Congress Catalog No. 87-082679

LANGTRY PUBLICATIONS
7838 Burnet Avenue
Van Nuys, CA 91405-1051

ISBN 0-915369-02-8 paper
ISBN 0-915369-03-6 hardcover
Printed in the United States of America

1 2 3 4 5 6 7 8 9 10

CALIFORNIA JUNIOR HERITAGE SERIES

The Indians and the California Missions

Father Junipero Serra the Traveling Missionary

Gold Rush Adventure

Available from:

Langtry Publications

7838 Burnet Avenue

Van Nuys, CA 91405-1051

ACKNOWLEDGMENTS

All the photographs in this book are reproduced courtesy of the California State Library. Special thanks go to the librarians for their time and care in researching these photographs. Line drawings are illustrated by Phyllis Garber except those by Graphic Products Corporation on p. 58 and 61. Any dialogue or quotations are not fictionalized but taken from diaries, letters or primary source material.

PREFACE

One of the most exciting times in American history was the California Gold Rush. Thousands of people came from all over the world to search for gold! They helped to settle the West.

I took a trip through the gold country and the old mining towns. It was exciting to imagine what life was like back then. I knew had to write a book about the gold seekers and their adventures.

Few factual books are written on this subject for elementary school children. I hope this book with its old photographs will help bring to life this time in California history.

Any dialogue or quotations used in this book are factual.

CONTENTS

GOLD RUSH ADVENTURE

John Sutter with Sutter's Fort in the background

1

JOHN SUTTER AND HIS FORT

The discovery of gold in California on January 24, 1848 happened by accident. The news created such excitement that thousands of people from all over the world rushed to California. They hoped to strike it rich! The California Gold Rush lasted less than ten years. The result would change California and the United States forever.

The story of the gold rush should begin with John Sutter and his settlement. He hired James Marshall, a worker, to build on land where the gold was found.

Sutter was born in Kandern, Germany on February 15, 1803 to Swiss parents. Little is known about his childhood. As a young man, he worked as a clerk in several shops before opening his own. When the shop failed, he fled his debts and sailed for America. Leaving behind a wife and four children, he hoped to send for them soon.

America offered Sutter a new start in life. The next five years he spent traveling throughout the United States. His journeys took him through Missouri, the Southwest, Mexico, Alaska, and Hawaii. He worked for a while as a trader on the Santa Fe Trail. Hearing exciting stories about California, he decided that was where he wanted to settle.

California belonged to Mexico in 1839 when Sutter first arrived. Most of the people living in California were Mexicans and Indians. The Mexicans had come as settlers. Their government agreed to give them large gifts of land called *land grants* to settle in this colony. They chose land along the coast to build their ranches.

Raising cattle was their chief economy and everything centered around it. They ate the beef and made products from the cattle. Scraping and tanning the hides; the workers crafted the leather into shoes, saddles, carpets, mats, and blankets. It was an easy way to make a living. There was plenty of time for lively celebrations of dances and *fiestas* or parties. These often lasted for days.

Many of the Indians worked on the ranches as cowboys, craftsmen, and servants. In earlier times they had lived on Spanish missions before their breakup. Other Indians further inland still lived in native villages. Much of California was wilderness.

Sutter came with a dream. He wanted to own land and build a settlement. He visited Juan Alvarado, the Mexican governor in California. Sutter asked him for land in the Sacramento Valley.

Governor Alvarado liked Sutter, who made friends easily. Alvarado realized the Mexican settlers did not want this land. It was too far inland away from the coast. Alvarado told Sutter he had to become a Mexican citizen and promise to work the land. Sutter agreed to do this. Alvarado gave him 50,000 acres of land.

Sutter named his land New Helvetia, which meant *New Switzerland* for his old country. It was a beautiful setting where trees and grass grew plentifully. Deer, antelope, ducks, and other wild animals roamed. Here the Sacramento and American Rivers met. The nearest ranch or town was fifty miles away.

First, Sutter built a house out of adobe bricks. He hired Indians and other workers to help him build it. They built a tall wall around it that was 18 feet high and 2½ feet thick. The wall surrounded 75,000 square feet. The building looked so much like a fort that people called it Sutter's Fort.

On some of the land he raised horses, mules, cattle, pigs, and sheep. His herds grew to thousands of animals. In the rich soil, he planted orchards of peach, apple, and fig trees. He grew fine crops of wheat, beans, cotton, and barley.

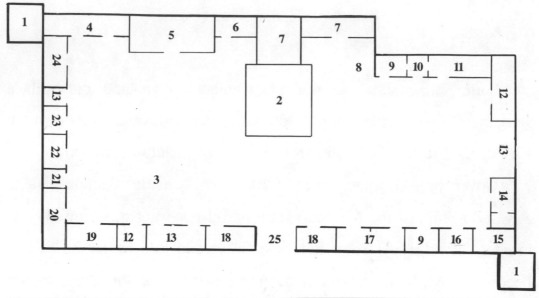

SUTTER'S FORT (inside)

1. Bastions & jails
2. Main building
3. Well
4. Brewery
5. Kitchen
6. Shoemaker Shop
7. Animal Corral
8. Bake Oven
9. Bakery
10. Trade Store
11. Weaving Room
12. Candle Room
13. Sleeping Rooms
14. Emigrant Rooms
15. Lumber Room
16. Saddlery
17. Granary
18. Guard Rooms
19. Blacksmith Shop
20. Gunsmith Shop
21. Coal Bin
22. Cowboys' Rooms
23. Hat & Boot Shop
24. Carpentry Shop
25. Gate

The fort was growing into a small community. Workshops and stores were built. Sleeping and storage rooms, a bakery, animal corrals, and a granary were also added.

Each day Sutter told the workers the tasks to be done. He trained men to serve as guards to protect the fort.

The noise of activity could be heard throughout the day. The clanging and hammering of workers rang out. People rode up on horseback wanting to buy, sell, or trade supplies. Wagon trains pulled up. Pioneers used the fort as rest stop when they reached California.

Sutter's Fort

People liked John Sutter. Everyone called him Captain Sutter, though he had never been a soldier. He always welcomed new settlers and offered them free food and shelter. Many stayed and worked for him. He constantly needed more people to make his settlement grow. Workers tended the fields, animals, and shops.

Already other foreigners had been coming to California. Ships sailed there from America, Spain, France, and England. Captains and sailors traded their goods for cattle hides and products.

American and English merchants had established trading posts or stores along the coast. They bought goods from the ships and sold them to the Californians. Many of these merchants married Mexican ladies and were given land grants.

American trappers and traders found routes on horseback over the plains, deserts, and mountains. American pioneers traveling west across the United States between 1841 and 1849 were coming to farm.

The Russians had built a fort. They used it for their fur-trapping business. When they closed Fort Ross in 1841, they sold it to Sutter. He bought the livestock, tools, buildings, weapons—everything for $30,000. This was considered a bargain. Sutter used the guns and cannons to protect the fort. He paid for them mainly on credit. It put him badly in debt.

The Mexican settlers were unhappy with the Mexican government. The settlers wanted to rule themselves. They complained about the laws, the government leaders, and the soldiers sent to protect them. Several times the settlers tried to overthrow the government in California. They failed.

Americans living in California wanted it to become part of the United States. Other countries, including the United States, realized Mexico could not rule California much longer.

On May 13, 1846, the United States declared war on Mexico. Separately, a group of Americans raised a flag in Sonoma on June 14th. They declared California a republic, free from Mexico. This was called the Bear Flag Revolt. They had not yet heard about the war. When Captain John C. Fremont told them, they joined the side of the United States. In 1848 the United States won the war. California was made a territory and later a state in 1850.

Meanwhile, Sutter's dream was coming true. His settlement was growing. He was becoming an important man in California. Many sailors and soldiers from the war stayed and worked for him. Many more American pioneers were coming to farm.

The population of California had grown to about 14,000 white people and 200,000 Indians.

What would the pioneers use to build their houses? Sutter wanted to sell them lumber. He needed a sawmill to cut the trees into wood. Sutter hired a carpenter named James W. Marshall to build and operate a sawmill.

James Marshall as a young man

sawmill

2

THE DISCOVERY OF GOLD

A crew of about a dozen workers hired on to help Marshall build the sawmill. Mormons, who had served as soldiers in the Mexican War, and Indians came. The Wimmer family joined them.

Marshall picked land next to the American River where plenty of trees grew. The Indians called the land Coloma. It was forty miles east of the fort in the wilderness.

The workers cut down trees to build the mill. But the hardest part was digging a ditch called a *race* from the river to the sawmill. Water from the river would flow up to the mill and turn the water wheel. The saws would cut the logs. The finished lumber would be floated down the river to the fort.

Work on the sawmill was coming along well. They had been digging the *race* deeper. On the morning of January 24, 1848, Marshall rose and walked down to inspect the men's work.

A shiny, yellow object caught his attention. Dipping his hand in the water, he brought out a piece of gleaming metal. Was it gold? Marshall was not sure. He pounded and flattened it with a rock. It bent like gold but did not break. He told his workers but they would not believe him. They thought it was fool's gold, a metal that looks like gold but is worthless.

Several days later Marshall rode on horseback to the fort, taking some samples of gold with him. When he arrived, he looked for Sutter. Marshall told him he had something important to say to him.

"Are you alone?" Marshall asked.

"Yes," replied Sutter.

"Did you lock the door?"

"No, but I will if you wish it," Sutter agreed.

Marshall asked for a scale. Drawing out his handkerchief, he unwrapped the gold. "I believe this is gold," he said, "but the people at the mill laughed and called me crazy."

"It certainly looks like it," Sutter replied.

Sutter performed tests on the metal. First, he pounded it with a hammer. Then he weighed it in water. He applied acid on it to see if it would rust. Finally, he was sure that the metal Marshall had found was really gold.

Would the workers be able to keep this secret? Sutter wanted his mill to be finished. He was afraid the workers would run off looking for gold. And he did not want more people coming.

How much gold was there? Sutter decided to visit the spot where the gold was found. The work crew in Coloma wanted to be sure he found gold. They gathered up all the gold they had already found and put it back in the *race*. This trick is called *salting a mine* or putting gold in it.

In a few days Sutter rode to Coloma. He was greeted by one of the Wimmer boys. Unknown to the workers, the boy had gathered up all the gold they had left for Sutter to find. Sutter was pleased with the gold and found more himself.

He talked to the men and gave them gifts of pocket knives. They agreed to keep the gold a secret for six weeks until the mill was finished. The men on their own time could look for gold and keep what they found. A man named Henry Bigler was the first *prospector* or gold hunter among them.

Meanwhile, Sutter visited the Indians who lived on the land and drew up a treaty. It said that Sutter could rent the land for three years. Nothing was mentioned to the Indians about the discovery of gold. He also sent a letter to Colonel Richard Mason, the new American governor in California. He turned down Sutter's request to own the land.

Something as exciting as this was too hard to keep secret! Henry Bigler wrote to his friends in the Mormon Battalion and told them about the gold. Even Sutter was not good about keeping the secret. He wrote to his friend, Mariano Vallejo.

A wagon driver named Jacob Wittmer, who delivered supplies, came to the mill. One of the Wimmer children told him about the gold. He didn't believe the boy. Mrs. Wimmer became so angry that her son was called a liar, she told the man the truth. She gave him a sample of gold dust. On his return to the fort, he stopped at the store owned by George Smith and Sam Brannan. He bought a drink with the gold.

People started talking about the rumors of gold in Coloma. Not many believed it. Six years before, Francisco Lopez had found gold near Los Angeles. It didn't amount to much. After a few years, it was gone. So people didn't take this rumor seriously.

The newspaper, *The Californian*, reported on March 15, 1848, the first story about the gold discovery.

GOLD MINE FOUND. In the newly made raceway of the Saw Mill recently erected by Captain Sutter, on the American Fork, gold has been found in considerable quantities. One person brought thirty dollars worth to New Helvetia, gathered there in a short time. California, no doubt, is rich in mineral wealth.

Some say it was Sam Brannan who stirred up all the excitement about gold. The storekeeper also published a newspaper, *The California Star.* Curious, he visited the sawmill to learn the truth. He found gold! This could boost business at the store. It was right on the way to the sawmill. Gathering up gold dust in a bottle, he rode to San Francisco. On May 12th, he ran up and down the streets shouting, "Gold! Gold! Gold from the American River!"

When people saw the gold, they believed it. What happened next was like a stampede. What excitement! Men left their plows, farms, and ranches. They stopped whatever they were doing and rushed to the gold fields.

Sam Brannan

The last issue of *The Californian* on May 29th said:

The whole country, from San Francisco to Los Angeles, and from the seashore to the Sierra Nevada, resounds to the sordid cry of Gold! Gold! Gold! While field is half planted, the house half built, and everything neglected but the manufacture of shovels and pickaxes.

The next day the editor, Mr. Buckelew, ran off to the gold fields to try his luck.

Sutter found his mill overrun with gold seekers. He tried getting them off the land but they wouldn't leave. His workers from the fort and sawmill began to leave. Work was left unfinished. Crops rotted in the fields and hides were left untanned. Sutter's settlement was doomed.

Californians caught the gold fever first. People of San Francisco emptied out of the town. They rented boats, rode horses, and walked to the land where gold was found. Up and down the coast of California people hurried to get to Coloma.

By April gold seekers from Sonoma, San Jose, Monterey, and Los Angeles were coming. Every town and ranch in California was buzzing with the news. Other towns were emptying of people. Some came from nearby Oregon or Sonora, Mexico. Over 5,000 people had arrived in the gold fields by summer.

California was still an isolated territory. It would be months before news reached the rest of the United States and other countries.

SEA ROUTES TO CALIFORNIA

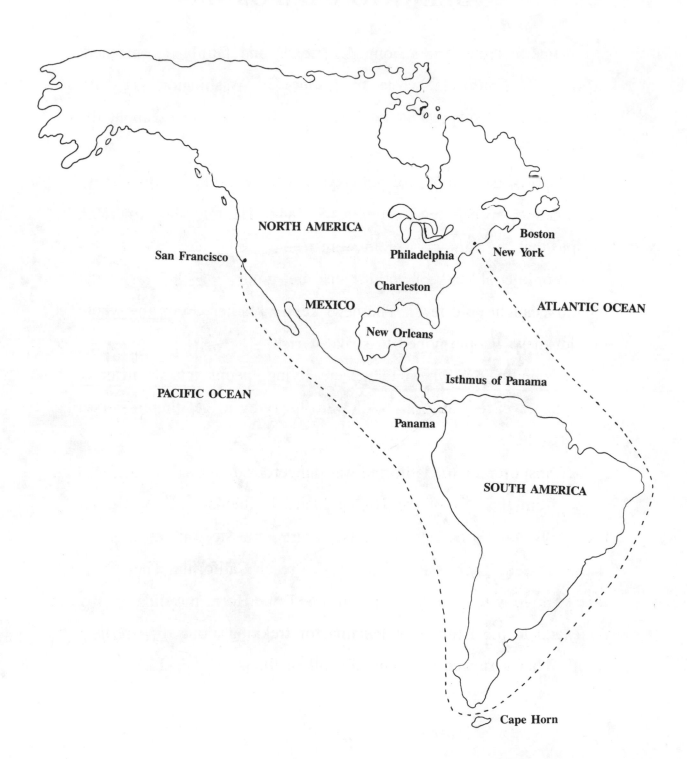

3
SAILING TO CALIFORNIA

Miners wrote letters home to friends and family. Government leaders in California wrote to leaders in Washington D.C. By September, newspapers in the East were printing stories about the gold discovery.

Reports and samples of gold reached the President, James Polk. He made a speech on December 5, 1848. He told the American people that the rumors of gold were true.

People could talk of nothing else but gold. Now the rest of the country caught gold fever. The news kept spreading. Soon the whole world knew. People hoped to strike it rich!

Depending on where they were living, people chose different ways to travel to California. All were hurrying to get there as soon as possible.

Transportation to California was dangerous and long. It was separated from the rest of the United States by thousands of miles of ocean. By land a barrier of plains, deserts, and steep mountains had to be crossed. There was no easy way to reach California. They chose one of three ways: sailing by ship around Cape Horn, traveling by ship and land to the Isthmus of Panama, or trekking along the overland trail. What a rugged adventure for all of them!

TRAVEL BY SHIP

The first ships left for California in November of 1848. By December people crowded aboard any ship sailing there. The gold rush had started! Most Easterners sailed by ship around Cape Horn for San Francisco. It took four to eight months, depending on the weather. This was the favorite route of the gold seekers.

As many ships as could be found were used. Some were rotted and in poor shape. Captains crowded too many people into them. Cargo ships meant for hauling goods were used as passenger ships.

The cost of one passenger ticket totalled three hundred dollars. About 40,000 people came by ship in the first few years. They left on the east coast from ports like New York, Boston, and Philadephia. Those from the South took off from New Orleans and Charleston. Not many women took these trips.

What did the gold seekers do to amuse themselves on such a long voyage? All day long for months they had to find a way to pass the time. Some fished and watched for whales and porpoises. They played cards and other games like checkers, backgammon, chess, and dominoes. Writing letters to loved ones at home and keeping diaries of the trip were popular activities. Reading helped to pass the time. Gambling, shooting bottles, and pitching pennies were among the many entertainments the bored passengers thought up.

On warmer days, they cleared the deck and danced. Passengers played the fiddle and sang songs. "The Banks of the Sacramento" was a favorite song. It was sung to the tune of "Camptown Races" by Stephen Foster.

> *A bully ship and a bully crew*
> *Dooda, dooda,*
> *A bully mate and a captain too,*
> *Dooda dooda day.*
> > *Chorus:*
> *Then blow ye winds hi-oh,*
> *For Californyo,*
> *There's plenty of gold so I've been told*
> *On the banks of the Sacamento.*

Those were the best parts of the voyage. Complaints of the passengers numbered many. Stormy weather tossed the ships about, waves breaking over the deck. Some ships sank and passengers drowned. The rolling seas made them seasick. Others caught scurvy, a disease caused by lack of fresh fruit in their diets.

The meals aboard were tasteless. Meat, vegetables, and bread were served. Sometimes the food and water was spoiled or they ran out of it altogether. Bugs got into their food and beds.

The cold, wet weather prevented them from staying out on deck. They got tired of being crowded, cooped up, and seasick down in the cabins. Passengers often quarreled with ship captains. For many reasons, gold seekers cheered when they sailed into San Francisco Bay.

Gold seekers traveling through the jungle

BY SEA AND LAND

The Isthmus of Panama Route was the quickest but most dangerous. It was first opened to speed up the delivery of mail between the east and west coasts of the United States. Gold seekers who wanted to travel faster boarded these clipper ships. The trip took three to five months. The ships left them off on the Chagres River in Panama.

From here, the gold seekers hired native people to take them in boats up the river to Gorgona. They charged high fees. Gold seekers could be stranded if they didn't have enough money. Others found bandits waiting to rob or kill them.

When the passengers could hire boats, they boarded *bungos*. Made from hollowed-out logs, they looked like canoes. The drivers drove long poles through the water to make the boats glide along.

The jungle they traveled through was filled with strange sights and sounds. Cries of monkeys, parrots, and alligators could be heard. Gold seekers had never seen anything like it.

At the end of this trip, the people still had to travel by land across to Panama City. They could travel over the mountains by mule or on foot. Those on foot had to watch out for snakes. The jungle heat weakened the travelers. Mosquitos stung them and gave many a disease called malaria. Others died of cholera and yellow fever.

Ships left from Panama City sailing for San Francisco. Gold hunters sometimes had to wait for weeks or months before catching a ship. Then they were bound for the gold fields at last!

Once they reached San Francisco, they took boats up the Sacramento or San Joaquin Rivers to reach the gold fields. Others packed their supplies on mules or horses and rode over the mountain trails. Some traveled by foot. They headed for mining camps already established or started new ones.

RUSH TO THE GOLD MINES FROM SAN FRANCISCO IN 1848.

4

BY OVERLAND TRAIL

That first spring of 1849, over 20,000 people were waiting to start the overland trip to California. They could not start until April or May when grass appeared for the cattle to eat along the trail. Then they could take four or five months to complete their journey before the snows of winter set in.

Most Americans living in the Midwestern states chose to travel overland. This cost less than any other way. Many of them were farmers who already owned horses, oxen, and wagons. People living in the city, who knew nothing about surviving in the wilderness, came along too.

Many people who traveled along the trail formed companies. They banded together in groups of wagon trains for protection. Some hitched up their horses or oxen to wagons and piled their possessions into them. Others rode horseback. Some walked the whole 1,800 miles.

The wagon trains moved out from St. Joseph and Independence, Missouri and Council Bluffs, Iowa. About 42,000 people came by land in the years of the gold rush.

The gold seekers kept diaries of their journeys. From reading these, we learn about their struggles.

OVERLAND ROUTES TO CALIFORNIA

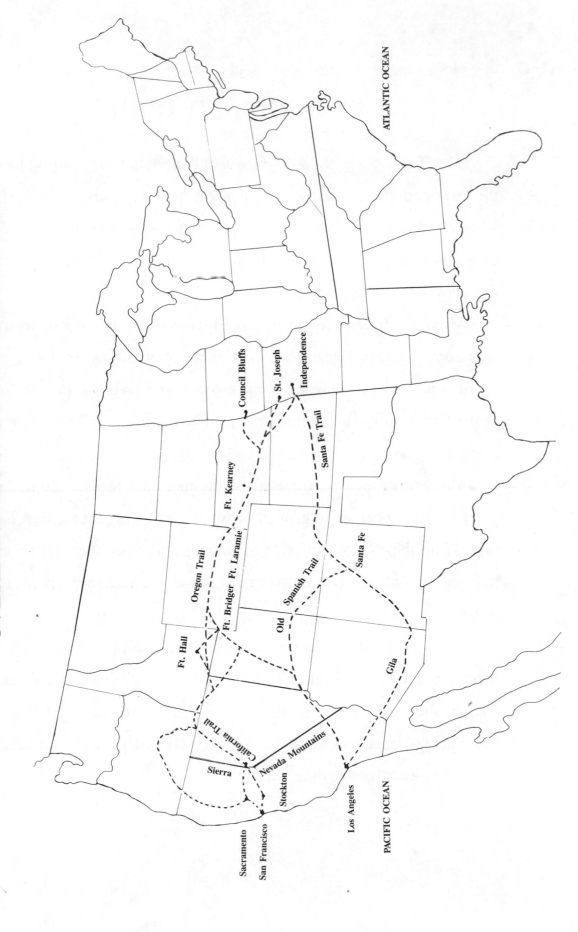

The trails they took were those blazed by the fur trappers and traders. The most commonly traveled trail was the Oregon Trail from Missouri west. At the mountains, they took the California Trail to Sutter's Fort. Another trail less traveled was the Santa Fe Trail to the Old Spanish Trail or the Gila Route. Among the passes used to get through the Sierra Nevada Mountains were Donner Pass, Emigrant Gap, Carson Pass, and Lassen's Cutoff. Sometimes they took other routes or short cuts and got lost.

It was a rough journey that took them across the plains, through hot deserts, and over the mountains. They had to cross swiftly moving rivers. Out in the open they constantly battled the rain, heat, and floods.

Hundreds of wagons crowded the trails to California. The heavy wagons moved slowly. Gold seekers traveled 15 to 20 miles a day. So many wagons rolled along that people and animals breathed the choking dust of those in front of them.

Men fished and hunted rabbits, deer, and buffalo for food. Other times they searched for game and water but could find none. Many died of hunger and thirst. Graves and skeletons of dead animals marked the trail.

They traveled through Indian land. But the Indians did not like them tramping through their land and killing their game. Sometimes Indians attacked them.

Sickness brought them hardships on the trail. Bad water and spoiled food made them ill. Catching more serious illnesses like dysentery, fever, scurvy, and cholera often resulted in death.

If the travelers started too late, the mountains would be covered with snow. Their jagged peaks could be dangerous and slippery to cross. The animals would not be able to find food.

The travelers knew about the Donner Party, pioneers trapped by the early snows of the Sierra Mountains. They remembered how so many had starved or died from the cold. They did not want to take the same chance. They knew they had to reach California before winter set in.

Along the trails it was not unusual to find abandoned clothing, furniture, and food. When the wagons could not bear the weight they carried, these objects were left behind.

Scouts rode ahead and searched for a place to camp for the night. By the time the sun went down, the travelers had drawn their wagons around in a circle at camp. The men tended to the animals and wagons, while a cook started supper. People were in trouble if their wagons broke down. They had to repair them themselves. If the animals died, they had to abandon their wagons. So they tried to take good care of them.

Around the campfire at night they ate, played cards, and strummed banjos and fiddles. They told stories and sang songs. Most went to bed early, while others took turns guarding the people and animals through the night.

People pitched tents to sleep in or slept near the wagons. They listened to wolves and other wild animals howling.

A favorite song they sang along the trail is still sung today. It tells of the hardships on the way.

Sweet Betsey From Pike

"Oh, don't you remember sweet Betsey from Pike,
Who crossed the big mountains with her lover Ike,
With two yoke of oxen, a large yellow dog,
A tall Shanghai rooster and one spotted hog.
Chorus:
Tooralai orralai ooralai a.

The Shanghai ran off, and their cattle all died,
That morning the last piece of bacon was fried;
Poor Ike was discouraged and Betsey got mad,
The dog dropped his tail and looked wondrously sad."

5

THE FORTY-NINERS

Who were the gold seekers? Most were young men in their early twenties, though older men came too. Few women came and fewer brought their families.

Because many came in 1849, gold seekers were called *forty-niners*. Bankers, farmers, ranchers, ministers, doctors, fur traders, businessmen, and people from every occupation came.

Most of the miners came from the United States. But news spread throughout the world. Eager people sailed from Australia, Europe, South America, Mexico, and China. A total of 85,000 people came in 1849. One fourth arrived from foreign countries.

Why did they come? People dreamed of becoming rich. They came looking for a better life. Many had left countries where they suffered from poverty, starvation, and war. Slavery was still legal in the South. Blacks came to earn money to buy their freedom or their family's. Free blacks were eager for a new start. Others sought adventure and excitement.

What supplies did the new miner need before going out to the gold fields? The work was grubby and hard. The clothes he picked were practical. Most wore red flannel shirts, brown pants, boots, and a hat. It was so common to see men wearing these clothes they became known as the uniform of the gold rush.

He needed to purchase food and mining equipment too. At first a pick, shovel, and metal pan was all he needed for panning gold. Later on the equipment changed and became more complicated. Pistols and a bowie knife served as protection.

When they arrived in California, miners were surprised to find out how much ordinary things cost. One egg cost $3, a pound of butter $6, candy $.50, flour $.40 a pound, and $2 for a loaf of bread. Shovels sold for $20-100, a blanket for $100, a horse from $10-100, and boots from $10-100. Clothing sold at twice the usual price. Prices varied with the mining town or camp. Store owners charged as high a price as anyone would pay.

Some store owners took advantage of the people who came. Owners made more money than most miners. Many businessmen made their fortunes in the food or supplies they sold the miners not in the gold fields. Sam Brannan, who helped spread the news of the gold rush, became a wealthy storekeeper.

A taylor named Levi Strauss came to California seeking his fortune. He brought denim cloth with him. Another miner asked him to sew a pair of pants for him. More miners bought the pants. That is how he started the company that still makes Levis jeans today.

A twenty-year-old man named Philip Armour earned money digging ditches in California. From his savings, he opened a butcher shop and sold beef to the miners. What a success he was!

The miners put up with the prices. They dreamed of "Seeing the Elephant." This popular saying meant going to California to look for gold and the problems that came with it. It is taken from a story about a farmer who wanted to see an elephant. He heard the circus was coming to town. Loading up his wagon with goods to sell at market, he started off. When his horse saw the elephant, it reared and turned over the wagon. It broke the eggs and bruised the man. The farmer was still happy because he saw an elephant.

Gold seekers felt much the same way. They risked everything, even their lives to search for gold!

Miners using a long tom and panning for gold

44

6
THE SEARCH FOR GOLD

Where did the new miners look for gold? They usually stopped first in Coloma, where James Marshall had discovered gold. Not many stayed there. It was already overcrowded with miners digging along the riverbank. So they rushed on to work other streams and rivers in the mountains. Some searched between the rocks and in dry stream beds.

Miners worked alone or with partners. Few had experience in mining. They read books on it but often learned from other miners in the *diggings* or gold fields. Mexican and Chilean miners proved the exception. Many possessed mining skills. The miners roamed from place to place in search of gold.

They found three forms of gold: gold dust, flakes, and nuggets. Gold dust looked like yellow sand. Flakes appeared a little bigger. Nuggets looked like small rocks of gold. The larger the size of the gold, the better. They carried it around in a small leather bag and used it like money to buy things.

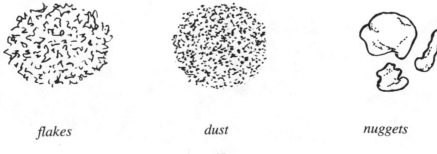

flakes   *dust*   *nuggets*

How did the gold get there? Rocks in the mountains contained gold. For thousands of years it was trapped. Rain, wind, and the flow of rivers over the rocks wore them down. The rocks broke up and freed the gold. The flow of the rivers moved it along. The gold settled in the bottom of rivers and streams. This gold was called free or *placer* gold. The first few years most of the gold mined was this kind.

The miners took along food, mining tools, and supplies. They packed them on their backs or on mules. Over the steep trails they climbed to reach the gold fields.

Along streams and riverbanks, miners worked with various tools to find gold. The clatter of picks and shovels against the rocks rang out.

PANNING FOR GOLD

At first, the ways of mining gold were simple. Only a pick, shovel, and a pan were needed.

A miner used a round pan made of iron or tin. The bottom was flat and the sides slanted. It measured 14–16 inches in diameter and 2½ to 3″ deep. At the river, the miner filled the pan with gravel, sand, and water from the bottom. He slanted the pan and swirled it around so the water and sand spilled out over the sides. Gold was heavy and sank to the bottom. If there was any, it was left behind in the pan with the gravel. Then gold could be easily picked out.

This was called *washing* the gold. Mostly gold dust and flakes were found. A lucky miner might find a nugget. The miner sampled several pans full as a test. If much *color* or gold was found, it was called *pay dirt*. Then he would decide to stay and *stake a claim*. If little or none was found, he would move on.

What tiring and uncomfortable work! The miner waded in cold water. He squatted down by the river while he panned gold. His leg and back muscles ached. The miner washed 50 to 100 pans of dirt a day. If he didn't have a pan, he used a tightly-woven Indian basket.

Panning was a slow method. The miner looked for new ways of getting the gold out faster. Many were surprised to find mining was such hard work.

STAKING A CLAIM

If the miner found enough gold, he would *stake a claim* or claim the land. How did he do this? It was simple. He left a mining tool like a pick or shovel on the spot he wanted to claim. Sometimes the miner had to write it down on paper and take it to the mining office. There it was recorded in a book.

Each mining camp made up its own rules about claims. The size of land they could mine varied. Claims ranged between 10 and 30 square feet. To keep a claim, the miner had to work it.

CRADLE

The cradle was a tool made from a hollowed-out log. It looked like a wooden box 3 or 4 feet long by 2 feet wide. On the top a smaller box with an iron bottom was placed. Holes were punched in it. The other end of the cradle was open with strips of wood nailed to the bottom. It stood on rockers.

This invention brought a change. Men working alone now worked with partners. Two to four people operated it. They placed it on the edge of a stream. One shoveled dirt from the stream bottom into the top. They poured buckets of water over it. Another person used the handle to rock the cradle.

Sand, gravel, gold, and water ran through the holes in the iron. Bigger stones stayed on top. The water and motion separated the gold from the rest. Water and sand ran out the open end. Gold was caught on the wooden strips at the bottom. Using it was faster than panning. Miners could wash out between 250 to 300 pans a day. Each day they divided up the gold.

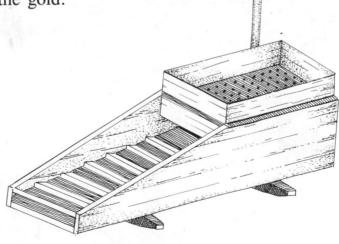

LONG TOM

The cradle lost too much gold. The miner wanted a tool that worked even faster. The long tom was longer than a cradle. It measured 10 to 20 feet long by 16 inches wide. It worked in a similar way.

It was placed in the stream so rushing water could run through it. Dirt was shoveled into the long part. As water flowed through it, an iron sheet punched with holes trapped the big rocks. Sand, gravel, and gold washed through the holes. A box underneath caught the gold.

The long tom could wash ten times more sand and gravel than a cradle. It saved time and work. Miners could wash 400-500 bucketfuls of dirt. But more miners were needed to work it. The cradle started to disappear when this was invented but not totally. The long tom needed a lot of running water and could not be used everywhere. The cradle was still used by miners working with fewer people.

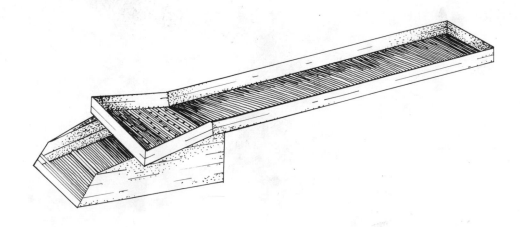

SLUICE BOX

The next invention became the sluice box. Miners built it by joining wooden boxes together. Longer than the long tom, it was built between 50 to 100 feet. All the boxes had wooden bars on the bottom to catch the gold.

Miners shoveled dirt into the boxes, while water ran through one end. Gold fell into the boxes. Quicksilver or mercury was sometimes added. The gold clung to it and trapped even the small grains. Later, the quicksilver could be heated and used again.

More miners joined in partnerships to work the sluice box. They guarded the boxes day and night from thieves. On Sundays they cleaned them out and took their share of gold. As with all these tools, they used the pan to wash out the last bit of gold.

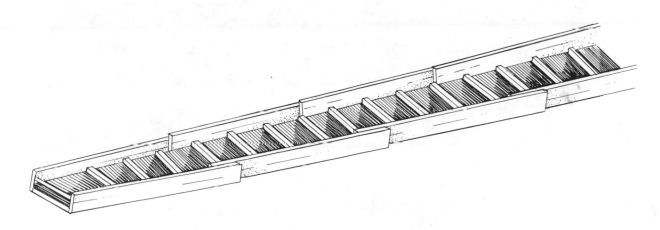

STRIKING IT RICH

Mining proved to be a gamble. Some people got lucky and found gold. Others did not. Rich gold strikes were often discovered by mistake.

Bennager Raspberry was having trouble with his rifle and fired it into the ground. It struck a piece of rock. That rock happened to have gold in it. In three days he took out $10,000 worth of gold from that spot and kept on finding a fortune.

A twelve-year-old boy named Davenport found $2,700 worth of gold in two days. In Sonora, a lump of gold was dug out of the main street on May 25, 1852. It was worth $1,173.

One of the largest nuggets ever found weighed 148 lbs. 8 ounces. Named the Monumental, it measured 15 inches long, 6 inches wide and 4 inches thick. Four Americans and one Swiss miner found it and sold it for $40,000.

Miners at the Big Bonanza Mine took out over $160,000 worth of gold.

Many men did not find enough gold to make more than $5 to 30 a day. Still, the miner hoped to make a fortune and gambled everything for it. Others wanted to leave but couldn't because they didn't have the money for the trip home.

7

LIFE IN A MINING TOWN

Mining towns sprang up overnight. They also died quickly. A town or camp developed around where miners were digging for gold. Towns lasted as long as the miners found gold. Tents served as houses for the miners, though some slept out under the stars. Miners moved from place to place in search of the richest gold. Usually, they built simple cabins if they stayed in the same town for a while. The first tent or building, other than the miners', was the general store. Towns that became more permanent later on built houses, a church, a fire-house, a saloon, a hotel, a bank, and shops.

Where were the mining towns? They were located high in the Sierra Nevada Mountains. Tucked away from cities, they were not easy to reach. Drivers loaded the supplies in wagons, hitching up mule teams to haul them in. These supplies came by steam ships all the way from the eastern United States.

The major gold area of the California Gold Rush was in Northern California. This narrow belt of land stretched 200 miles long from Mariposa to Downieville (see map). The towns richest in gold were located between Auburn and Bear Valley. This was called the *mother lode*, which meant gold-rich area.

Miners chose humorous and colorful names for the towns. Flea Town, Poker Flat, and Hangtown described what these towns were known for. The towns named for animals included Rattlesnake Diggings and Bear Valley. Grass Valley and Sierraville were named for the land. Chinese Camp and Dutch Flat stood for the races or countries where the miners came from.

Marysville and Elizabethtown took their names from women the miners knew back home. Rough and Ready was named for an American hero, General Zachary Taylor. Murphys took its name from the man whose rich gold strike put that town on the map.

Not all the names lasted. Many of the strange ones later were changed.

CALIFORNIA MINING TOWNS

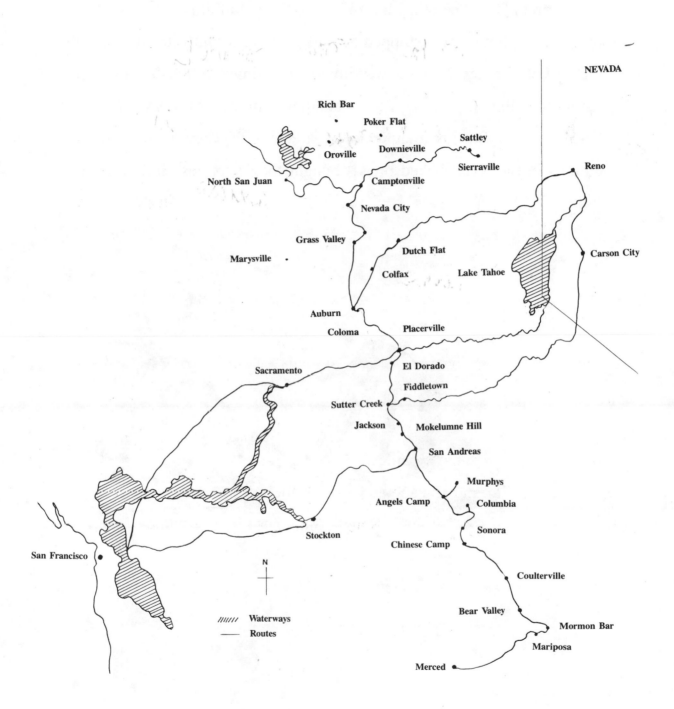

NEVADA

Rich Bar

Poker Flat

Sattley

Downieville

Oroville

Sierraville

Reno

North San Juan

Camptonville

Nevada City

Grass Valley

Dutch Flat

Marysville

Colfax

Lake Tahoe

Carson City

Auburn

Placerville

Coloma

Sacramento

El Dorado

Fiddletown

Sutter Creek

Mokelumne Hill

Jackson

San Andreas

Murphys

Angels Camp

Columbia

Sonora

Stockton

Chinese Camp

San Francisco

Coulterville

Bear Valley

Mormon Bar

Mariposa

Merced

N

////// Waterways
——— Routes

The miners woke up early in the morning, arose, and fixed themselves breakfast. Then they headed off to the gold fields. They worked hard all day long. Most stopped for lunch then continued to work until the end of the day. On their way home, sometimes they fished or shot game for dinner. Six days a week they worked, Monday through Saturday. On Sunday they enjoyed a day off. They washed their clothes in the river, baked bread, bought their supplies, and relaxed.

Over a campfire they cooked their meals using a frying pan and a pot. Their food was not very tasty or healthy. They fixed themselves plenty of pork, beans, and dried beef. They baked bread every week and flipped their pancakes in the frying pan on Sundays. Fresh beef, potatoes, and dried fruit were eaten less often. They drank coffee. A tin of sardines was considered a treat. Occasionally, they caught or bought fish or wild game. Fresh fruit and vegetables were almost impossible to find.

At night the miners would entertain each other by telling stories about gold and home. A banjo or a fiddle livened up a lonely night. Sometimes they would sing songs or play cards. Many kept dogs and mules as pets. Others caught wild animals and tried to tame grizzy bear cubs, squirrels, and raccoons.

Most of the miners hung around the general store. It was a natural meeting place. Gathering to swap stories, they spent many hours. Letters from home were read over and over again.

The miners worked hard and behaved like a roaring bunch of men on Sundays. It was their day of seeking entertainment. Sometimes they got drunk. They were lonely for home.

The saloon, at first, was the only social gathering place besides the general store. They spent their hard-earned money gambling and drinking. They cheered and bet on horse and dog races, bullfights, and bull-and-bear fights. Shooting contests and foot races were held. Dances were staged, though there were few women.

Bigger towns built theatres. By the 1850's there was much entertainment. Stagecoaches traveled to the larger mining towns. Circuses, acting groups, and singers visited. With them came more women.

Winter changed life at the mines. It rained heavily in the towns further north. Miners couldn't work. Many moved to San Francisco, Sacramento, and Stockton until the weather cleared. Further south, it rained less and more people stayed in the mines. Those without much money also stayed in the camps.

Mining towns could be dangerous. Miners carried guns and knives to protect themselves. At first there was not much crime. Later on when so many thousands of people swarmed to California, it became a problem.

Every mining camp or town set up rules to live by. Each town made its own laws. With no jails or policemen, the miners had to organize a system of justice.

They followed a democratic process. Robberies, murders, and land claims numbered among the problems to be settled. Court took place in the general store. A judge and jury was immediately selected. The person accused was tried by the other miners. Sometimes the storekeeper served as judge. Thieves were punished by whipping or ordered to leave town. People who committed murder usually faced hanging. One town was so rough and wild, the miners named it Hangtown for all the hangings that took place.

Other common problems with the law included quarrels over gold mining claims. As in other cases, the majority vote of the miners ruled.

Not all people received justice. Many Americans did not want to share any gold with people who had come from other countries. They did not feel foreigners had any right to it. Most immigrants lived in their own mining camps and kept to themselves. Sometimes Americans would treat them badly and even chase them off rich diggings.

In 1850, the Americans passed a law called the Foreign Miners' Tax. This law made the foreign miners pay $20 a month for hunting for gold. Some who had not found gold could not pay. Many went home. There were other prejudices. Many Indians, whose land was taken from them, were looked down upon and murdered. Americans took their claims and ran them off.

Fire swept quickly through a mining town. With only volunteer fire departments to fight the fires, it took longer. Most mining towns burned down at least once and had to be rebuilt. When the citizens rebuilt, they often used brick because it didn't burn. That is why some mining towns left today have brick buildings.

The weather was either too hot or cold. The miners got wet and cold working in rivers and stream beds. Their diet lacked good nutrition. These conditions combined with the hard, physical work of mining made many miners sick. They suffered from rheumatism, cholera, dysentery, scurvy, food poisoning, typhoid, tuberculosis, small pox, and general aches and pains.

Many of the miners took care of themselves and their friends when they got sick. Doctors charged high fees if any could be found in their mining camp. They treated those who could afford to pay them. Many miners died of diseases and also from gold mining accidents.

8

WOMEN AND OTHER ADVENTURERS

Few women came at first to the gold rush. Men stopped and stared when a new woman came to town. She was always welcomed and surrounded by men. Around 1850 less than eight percent of the population were women.

Mrs. Eliza Farham decided to do something about the lack of women in California. She placed an advertisement in several New York newspapers. Young ladies interested in marriage to miners were asked to write in. Many did but only a few wanted to make the journey. Miners were looking for women to marry too. Still, few women came.

An exception to this was Louise Clappe, nicknamed Dame Shirley. She traveled from the East with her husband, Dr. Fayette Clappe. They came to California for his health and moved to the town of Rich Bar.

She wrote letters to her sister back home. Telling colorful stories about the happenings in a California mining town, she described what life was like for a woman. Soon the editors of *Pioneer Magazine* and the *Marysville Herald* published her letters written between 1851 and 1852. *The Shirley Letters* have been published as a book and are still famous today.

As time passed, California was becoming less isolated because of better transporation. Faster clipper ships made the journey from the East to California much easier. Stagecoaches bumped over the rough roads to larger mining towns. A railroad was built across Panama.

Now people were coming to California for other reasons than to search for gold. Women were coming with their families to join their husbands or to marry. Both men and women were arriving to launch entertainment careers, start businesses, and become writers, painters, and photographers.

Women and children at the Union Hill Mine

Entertainers arrived in large numbers. Men and women, who came to entertain the miners, could make a great deal of money if they were talented. Performers could sing, dance, act, and play musical instruments. The miners wanted variety. These noisy miners clapped and cheered loudly when they enjoyed a performance. They threw bags of gold dust on stage. When they didn't like a performer, they booed and hissed them off stage.

A well-known entertainer and adventurer of her day named Lola Montez sailed from Europe to California. Part owner in the Eureka Gold Mine, she traveled to Grass Valley to live closer to it. The whole town turned out to greet her. At first, she was warmly welcomed by the miners. They enjoyed her dancing and singing performances, especially her spider dance. Later they tired of her lack of talent.

Among those who came to California to join their husbands was a woman named Mary Ann Crabtree. She brought her young daughter, Lotta, with her. They traveled to San Francisco. Lotta was fascinated by the groups of traveling actors swarming into the city. Her mother signed her up for dance classes.

Lola Montez took an interest in six-year-old Lotta Crabtree. She saw her talent and appeal as a child actor. She taught her some of her dances. Lola was joining a group of actors who were performing in Australia. She wanted Lotta to come along but Mrs. Crabtree was against it.

Lola Montez, entertainer, dance teacher, and part owner in the Eureka Gold Mine

Mrs. Crabtree decided to tour the mining camps with Lotta performing. A new teacher helped Lotta develop her singing, dancing, and acting performances. The miners loved Lotta. They would shower the stage with gold after her performances. Her mother carefully saved the money. Lotta's career grew. As Lotta became more famous, she played theatres in New York and foreign countries.

Lotta Crabtree

Another person who came during the gold rush was Mammy Pleasant, a free black woman. She was born a slave of a black mother and a Cherokee Indian father. A farmer bought her when she was a young girl. He educated her when he realized how smart she was. While at school, she met a black businessman and married him. Together they tried to help their people escape slavery.

When she heard about the gold rush, she decided to go to San Francisco. She became a cook and worked for high pay. When she decided to go into business for herself, she opened up a boarding house. She was successful and spent much of her money helping poor black people of the South.

Mammy (Mary Ellen) Pleasant

Newspaper reporters, writers, and publishers arrived in California. They wrote stories for newspapers about the miners and the gold rush. Most of the larger towns printed a newspaper.

Two writers who came to California were Samuel Clemens and Bret Harte. They told stories about the miners, their lives, and the mining towns. They sold them to newspapers. People living in the East and Midwest were always eager to read stories about the gold rush.

Bret Harte moved to California in 1854. He taught school and held a variety of jobs. Writing for newspapers and magazines; Harte created short stories and poems about the miners, gamblers, and women of gold rush country. "The Luck of the Roaring Camp" and "Outcasts of Poker Flats" were two of his most popular stories. While in California, he met and helped Samuel Clemens improve his writing and get published.

Samuel Clemens under the name Mark Twain wrote "The Jumping Frog of Calaveras County" and "Roughing It." The first one was about a frog-jumping contest. The mining town, Angel's Camp, still holds a frog-jumping contest once a year. "Roughing It" described his adventures in the mining camp. Later he wrote *The Adventures of Huckleberry Finn* and *The Adventures of Tom Sawyer*.

Both writers became famous and moved out of California. They drew their colorful and entertaining stories from their experiences in California throughout their lives.

Bret Harte was a famous writer

Samuel Clemens wrote under the name Mark Twain

9

CHANGING TIMES

In the beginning years of the gold rush, miners found only placer gold. This was on top of the ground and could be dug out with picks and shovels. With so many people searching for gold, most of this kind had been found by 1854.

More gold lay buried deeper in the ground. How could the miners get it out? They needed heavy machinery to dig it out. Only large companies had enough money to buy and operate the machines.

This marked a big change in mining. The day of the individual miner was over. Miners hired on with big mining companies to work for pay. Any gold they found belonged to the companies, not to them.

Hydraulic mining was a type of mining that could get loose gold out from underground. The powerful water hoses that were used looked like huge fire hoses. Workers chose a hillside and directed the water against it. The force of the water tore away sand, gravel, and rock. The gold could be separated from the rest. Great amounts of water were needed. Routes of streams and rivers were changed to get the water where it was needed. This ripped up the land and ruined it. Laws were passed to stop it.

Hydraulic mining

Another kind of gold was discovered trapped in solid rock. This was called *quartz* or *lode* gold. It was buried deep in the ground. Miners dug tunnels in hillsides or holes in the earth with machines. They dragged out the rock and put it in a machine called a *stamp mill*. It crushed the rock into powder. The gold was separated by washing it in water and quicksilver.

After placer mining dried up, some miners turned to crime. Other Indians, Californians, and foreigners sought revenge for the way some Americans had treated them. Criminals also had swarmed to California along with the stampede of gold seekers.

During the 1850's, gangs of outlaws roamed the countryside robbing and murdering. Many people did not feel safe. The government did not do much about the problem. So citizens formed groups called *vigilantes*. They captured criminals and punished them themselves. It was not a good practice. People felt they had no choice. Law and order came slowly to the new state.

No outlaws were more feared than Juaquin Murrieta and his gang. Many stories told about Murrieta make him seem like a hero. It is difficult to learn the truth. Legend says his family's land was taken away from them by the Americans. As a Mexican, he could have suffered bad treatment in the mines. But he and his gang murdered and stole from many miners throughout the gold country. No one felt safe. Finally, a Texas Ranger named Harry Love shot and killed him.

Gradually the towns started to calm down. Sheriffs were hired and courts upheld the law. The more families that came, the more settled towns seemed to get. Towns built churches and schools.

As more people came, the demand for land grew. Americans came to start farms. *Squatters* or people who settled on land not belonging to them objected to the large amounts of land owned by Mexican citizens. Mexican ranchers wanted these people off their land.

Congress decided to look closely at all claims to the land. It set up a committee in 1851. The owner had to prove his right to the land. This meant hiring lawyers and spending much time and money searching for important papers. The original grants were given so long before. Sometimes they were lost or never written down at all. As a result, many Mexican ranchers lost their land.

Though many people were still coming into California, others were leaving. With the giving out of the placer gold, some miners returned home. Those who still wanted to mine swarmed to other states like Nevada, Oregon, Idaho, Montana, Arizona, Colorado, and Dakota territory where news of gold and silver strikes gave them new hope. Some even traveled to Australia or British Columbia, Canada.

Those who stayed in California needed to look for a new way of making a living. Some took up farming or started businesses. Others worked for big mining companies.

With mining towns emptying of people, stores in those towns closed down. This led to *ghost towns* or deserted towns where no one lived. Other towns became farming towns or kept growing into big cities.

10
THE END OF THE GOLD RUSH

The gold rush lasted less than a decade. It began in 1848 and ended around 1856. This exciting time in American history brought sweeping changes for the country.

The gold rush caused a quick population growth for California. People swarmed to the state between 1848 and 1860. At the beginning of 1848 the population, not counting Indians, was 14,000. By the end of the gold rush, there were nearly 400,000 people.

It brought the state of California out of isolation. The demand for better transportation to the gold fields brought improvements. Routes overland to California were found earlier. The demand for faster ships to carry mail and passengers brought clipper ships. Stagecoach routes to the West were found. A railroad built in Panama connected the east and west coasts of the United States. Later a railroad across the United States was built.

Statehood came much sooner for California because of the California Gold Rush. The promise of gold and so many Americans living in the state gave it a better chance. In only two years it was admitted as the thirty-first state.

Gold created wealth for some people and the state as a whole. For those who struck it rich, some used it wisely. Others just gambled it away.

How much gold was found during the gold rush years? About $465 million was taken out from 1848 to 1856. The first year, 10 million dollars worth of gold was found. Each year after that between 40 and 60 million dollars worth was found.

Since many people stayed in California after the gold rush, the state was settled faster. Mining companies still continued to mine but for most people it was the beginning of the farming period in California history. People settled in other parts of California and built more towns.

Cities like Sacramento, San Francisco, and Stockton grew. San Francisco became a world sea port. More banks, restaurants, hotels, houses, schools, and churches were built.

Not everyone benefited from the gold rush. There were people who suffered and died trying to get to California. The two people who should have profited from the gold discovery both died in poverty.

Marshall tried to look for gold but never could find much after his big discovery. He sold his autograph, gave speeches, and lived on a small pension from the state government.

Sutter lost all of his land. To pay his debts, he had to sell off the fort and much of his land. Squatters went to court and took a second land grant away, Hock Farm. He tried gold mining but failed. In the first state election he ran for governor of California but lost. It was difficult for him to live on the small amount of money the state government gave him. In 1880 he died a poor and broken man.

None suffered more than the California Indians who lived around the gold fields. Americans swarmed over their land using it for mining or farming. They trampled their food supply. Many Indians were killed or run off their land.

Some turned to crime against these white men. They took their livestock and set fire to houses. The United States military troops battled with the Indians. Then the government made peace with the Indians. They signed treaties that gave them land. The Indians agreed to live on land called reservations.

Many of the towns that had boasted of a large population of gold seekers are today deserted. Their memories live on in history books, old buildings, and museums. They serve as reminders of the great California Gold Rush adventure.

IMPORTANT DATES IN
CALIFORNIA GOLD RUSH HISTORY

August, 1839—John Sutter arrives in California.

November 4, 1841—The first group of American pioneers with leader, John Bidwell arrive in Northern California.

March, 1842—Francisco Lopez finds gold in the San Fernando Valley near Los Angeles. A small rush for gold occurs.

Spring of 1844—Capt. John C. Fremont's party of soldier-explorers come to California.

July, 1845—James Marshall arrives in California at Sutter's Fort.

May 13, 1846—The U.S. declares war against Mexico.

June 14, 1846—Americans in a revolt against the Mexican government stage the Bear Flag Revolt in Sonoma.

January 13, 1847—The Mexican War ends with the U.S. winning.

January, 1847—The Mormon Battalion reaches California. The fighting is already over.

January 24, 1848—John Marshall finds gold in the race of the sawmill.

March 15, 1848—*The Californian*, a San Francisco newspaper, is first to print the story of the gold discovery.

May 12, 1848—Sam Brannan runs through the streets of San Francisco announcing the gold discovery.

November, 1848—The first ships leave the East coast sailing for California with gold seekers aboard.

December 5, 1848—President Polk tells the nation the truth about the gold discovery.

April or May, 1849—The first wagon trains set out from Missouri and Iowa to travel by land to California.

October, 1849—People from Europe start traveling to California.

November 13, 1849—A state constitution is drawn up in California and government leaders are elected.

April, 1850—Foreign Miners' Tax is passed charging foreigners $20 a month for the right to mine gold.

September 9, 1850—California is admitted as the 31st state of the United States.

February, 1851—The first quartz mine is discovered in Amador Creek.

March 14, 1851—The Foreign Miners Tax is struck down.

March, 1851—The Land Commission is established.

March, 1853—Hydraulic mining begins.

Summer, 1853—Lola Montez, an entertainer, comes to Grass Valley.

Spring, 1854—Writer, Bret Harte, arrives in California.

Summer, 1854—Lotta Crabtree begins her entertainment career.

Summer, 1861—Samuel Clemens (Mark Twain) arrives in California.

June 18, 1880—John Sutter dies in poverty.

August 10, 1885—James Marshall dies.

WHERE TO WRITE
FOR FURTHER INFORMATION

Amador County Chamber of Commerce
P.O. Box 596
30 S. SR 49
Jackson, CA 95642

Auburn Area Chamber of Commerce
1101 High St.
Auburn, CA 95603

Calaveras County Chamber of Commerce
P.O. Box 111
753 S. Main St.
Angels Camp, CA 95222

Coulterville Chamber of Commerce
P.O. Box 333
Coulterville, CA 95311

El Dorado County Chamber of Commerce
542 Main St.
Placerville, CA 95667

Grass Valley Chamber of Commerce
248 Mill St.
Grass Valley, CA 95945

Mariposa County Chamber of Commerce
P.O. Box 425
Mariposa, CA 95338

Nevada City Chamber of Commerce
132 Main St.
Nevada City, CA 95945

Tuolumne County
P.O. Box 277
19445 Stockton Rd.
Sonora, CA 95370

PLACES TO VISIT IN GOLD COUNTRY

Amador County Museum
225 Church St.
Jackson, CA 95642

A variety of exhibits on mining include working models.

Angels Camp
Fairgrounds
Angels Camp, CA 95222

The Frog Jumping Jubilee is held yearly on the third week of May.

Columbia State Historic Park
P.O. Box 151
Columbia, CA 95310

The whole town is preserved to look like the a gold rush town.

El Dorado County Historical Museum
Fairgrounds
Placerville, CA 95667

The displays include a stagecoach.

Empire Mine State Historic Park
Empire St.
Grass Valley, CA 95945

One of the oldest and richest gold mines in California.

Hangtown's Gold Bug Park
Bedford Park
Placerville, CA 95667

Visitors can see mining equipment and explore a mine tunnel.

Indian Grinding Rock State Historic Park
Pine Grove-Volcano Rd.
Volcano, CA 95689

State park on Indians includes mortars, displays, and exhibits.

Mariposa County Museum and History Center.
12th & Jessie Streets
Mariposa, CA 95338

A good collection of relics from various periods of California history.

Marshall Gold Discovery State Park
310 Back St.
Coloma, CA 95613

A monument, museum, displays, and a working model of a sawmill.

North Star Powerhouse Mining Museum
S. Mill St.
Grass Valley, CA 95945

One of the best mining museums for mining methods and displays.

Northern Mariposa County History Center
Wells Fargo Building
Coulterville, CA 95311

Exhibits of a model of a stamp mill, tools, and photographs.

Placer County Historical Museum
1273 High St.
Auburn, CA 95603

Excellent museum of this time.

Sutter's Fort State Historic Park
2701 L St.
Sacramento, CA 95816

Audio self-guided tour of reconstructed fort.

Tuolumne County Museum
158 W. Bradford Ave.
Sonora, CA 95370

Clothing, photographs, and displays housed in the former jail.

GLOSSARY

adobe sun-dried bricks made of clay earth, straw, and water.

bastion part of a fort that stands above the rest.

battalion a company of soldiers.

brewery a place where liquor is made.

bungos small boats.

claim land marked by a miner as his.

color gold.

cradle a mining tool built on rockers and used to get out gold.

dam a wall built to hold back water.

diary a written record.

diggings the gold fields.

dirt sand and gravel which might contain gold.

dust tiny grains of gold.

emigrant a person who leaves one country to settle in another.

flake a chip.

flume a channel built for water to flow through.

forty-niners a name for gold seekers who came during the California gold rush.

ghost town a deserted town.

gold fever the excitement of gold.

granary a room or building for storing grain.

hydraulicking a mining method using water hoses to wash gravel hillsides to find gold.

immigrant a person who comes to a foreign country.

isthmus a thin strip of land connecting two larger pieces of land.

land grant a gift of land given by the Mexican government.

long tom a wooden trough 10 to 20 feet long by 16 inches wide used to mine gold.

merchant a trader or businessman.

mercury a metallic element that clings to gold.

Mormon a member of the Church of Latter-day saints.

mother lode land that is rich in gold.

nugget a lump of gold.

overland traveling by land.

panning using a pan, dirt, and water to separate the gold.

pass a narrow opening in the mountains.

pay dirt a name for dirt with gold in it.

pioneer one who settles in a new land.

placer gold gold found on the ground in streams and rivers.

prospector gold hunter.

quartz or **lode mining** gold found deep in the ground in bedrock.

race ditch in the raceway of a sawmill.

republic democracy.

reservation land set aside by the U.S. government.

saloon a bar.

salting a mine planting gold purposefully where there is none.

sawmill a mill used to saw logs into boards.

seeing the elephant saying used to describe the adventure of hunting for gold.

settlement land newly colonized.

shaft a long passage leading to the surface.

sluice box a mining tool similar to a cradle but longer.

squatter a person living on land that does not belong to them without the owner's permission.

stake a claim putting a marker in the ground to claim ownership of the land.

stamp mill a mill built to break up rocks containing gold.

strike the discovery of a large amount of gold.

territory land belonging to the U.S. government but not a state.

trapper a person who kills animals for the fur and sells them.

washing gold see panning.

worked out land from which all the gold is thought to be taken.

BIBLIOGRAPHY

Adler, Jack. *Exploring Historic California*. Pasadena: The Ward Ritchie Press, 1974.

American Heritage. *The California Gold Rush*. New York: Harper & Row, 1961.

Bancroft, Hubert Howe. *The Works of Hubert Howe Bancroft; History of California*, Vol. VI. 1848-1859. San Francisco: The History Company, Publishers, 1888.

Barker, Charles Albro, Editor. *Memoirs of Elisha Oscar Crosby; Reminiscences Of California and Guatemala From 1849 to 1864*. San Marino: Huntington Library, 1945.

Bigler, Henry. *Bigler's Chronicle of the West*. Berkeley: University of California Press, 1962.

Bryant, Edwin. *What I Saw In California*. New York: D. Appleton and Company, 1848.

Bruff, J. Goldsborough. *Gold Rush: The Journals, Drawings, and Other Papers of J. Goldsborough Bruff*. New York: Columbia University Press, 1944.

Canfield, Chauncey L. *The Diary of a Forty-niner*. New York: Houghton-Mifflin, 1920.

Clappe, Louise (Dame Shirley). *The Shirley Letters; Being Letters Written In 1851-1852 from the California Mines*. Santa Barbara: Peregrine Smith, 1970.

Colton, Walter. *Three Years In California 1846-1849*. New York: A. S. Barnes & Company, 1850.

Coy, Owen C., PhD. *In the Diggings in Forty-nine*. Los Angeles: The California State Historical Association, 1948.

Egenhoff, Elisabeth L. *The Elephant As They Saw It*. San Francisco: California Journal of Mines and Geology, 1949.

Gudde, Erwin G. *Sutter's Own Story; The Life of General John Augustus Sutter and the History of New Helvetian in the Sacramento Valley*. New York: Putnam's, 1936.

Johnson, William Weber. *The Forty-niners*. New York: Time-Life, 1974.

Packard, Major Wellman. *Early Emigration to California*. Fairfield: Ye Galleon Press, 1971.

Quaife, Milo Milton. *Pictures of Gold Rush California*. New York: The Citadel Press, 1967.

Scharmann, H.B., translated from German by Margaret Hoff Zimmerman and Erich W. Zimmermann. *Scharmann's Overland Journey To California; From the Pages of a Pioneer's Diary*. Freeport: Books for Libraries Press, 1918.

Stein, R. Conrad. *The Story of The Gold At Sutter's Mill*. Chicago: Childrens Press, 1981.

Twain, Mark. *Roughing It*. New York: Harper & Row, 1871.

Upham, Samuel C. *Notes Of a Voyage To California Via Cape Horn*, together with *Scenes In El Dorado In the Years 1849-50*: New York: Arno Press, 1973.

Webster, Kimball. *The Gold Seekers of '49; a Personal Narrative of the Overland Trail and Adventures in California and Oregon from 1849 to 1854*. Manchester: Standard Book Company, 1917.

White, Lonnie J. and Gillaspie, William R., Editors. *By Sea To San Francisco 1859-50: The Journal of Dr. James Morison*. Memphis: Memphis State University Press, 1977.

Zauner, Phyllis and Lou. *California Gold; Story of the Rush to Riches*. Sacramento: Zanel Publications, 1980.

INDEX

ABOUT THE AUTHOR

Linda Lyngheim is a California history enthusiast. She has written two other books for children on California history, *The Indians and the California Missions* and *Father Junipero Serra the Traveling Missionary*. Writing for adults, she has authored books and magazine articles. She received her Bachelor of Arts degree in social science from California State University, Fresno and an M.L.S. degree in library science from University of Southern California. As a librarian, she has worked for the Glendale Public Library and the Los Angeles Public Library.

ABOUT THE ILLUSTRATOR

Phyllis Garber is a graduate of Carnegie Mellon University. She studied at the Pittsburgh Art Institute and Pasadena School of Art. This is the third book she has illustrated for children. As a painter, she has received many local art awards for her watercolors. She resides in Laguna Beach.